DINOSAURS!

LESOTHOSAURUS
AND OTHER DINOSAURS AND REPTILES FROM
THE LOWER JURASSIC

by
David West

Gareth Stevens
Publishing

Please visit our website, www.garethstevens.com.
For a free color catalog of all our high-quality books,
call toll free 1-800-542-2595 or fax 1-877-542-2596.

Library of Congress Cataloging-in-Publication Data

West, David, 1956-
Lesothosaurus and other dinosaurs and reptiles from the lower jurassic / David West.
p. cm. — (Dinosaurs!)
Includes index.
ISBN 978-1-4339-6717-7 (pbk.)
ISBN 978-1-4339-6718-4 (6-pack)
ISBN 978-1-4339-6715-3 (library binding)
1. Dinosaurs—Juvenile literature. 2. Reptiles, Fossil—Juvenile literature. 3. Paleontology—Jurassic—
Juvenile literature. I. Title.
QE861.5.W47 2012
567.9—dc23
2011029449

First Edition

Published in 2012 by
Gareth Stevens Publishing
111 East 14th Street, Suite 349
New York, NY 10003

Copyright © 2012 David West Books

Designed by David West Books

Special thanks to Dr. Ron Blakey for the map on page 4

Printed in China

CPSIA compliance information: Batch #DW12GS: For further information contact Gareth Stevens, New York, New York at 1-800-542-2595.

Contents

The Lower Jurassic Period

The Lower Jurassic period began after the **mass extinction event** that ended the Triassic period. Life slowly recovered on land and in the seas as the oxygen levels began to increase. The carbon dioxide levels improved since their drastic low in the Triassic, creating a warming climate. The supercontinent, Pangaea, was breaking up, giving rise to what is now the Atlantic Ocean.

Dinosaurs lived throughout the Mesozoic Era, which is divided into three periods, shown here. It is sometimes called the Age of Reptiles. Dinosaurs first appeared in the Upper Triassic period and died out during a mass extinction event 65 million years ago.

More types of **pterosaurs** appeared while **plesiosaurs** and **ichthyosaurs** ruled the seas.

THE WORLD DURING THE LOWER JURASSIC
New bodies of water produced moist winds that brought rain to formerly dry, desert-like regions. Instead of severe heat, many areas started to experience comfortably warm conditions. Evidence of widespread coral reefs also suggests the atmosphere was becoming moist and **temperate** or tropical, providing the perfect conditions for animal and plant life. Compared to the Triassic, the Jurassic became far more lush and green. Pines, giant sequoias, and **monkey puzzle trees** grew along with palm-like **cycads** and **ginkgoes**. Ferns and horsetails grew in large amounts, becoming the main food for the expanding population of dinosaurs.

227	200	180	159	144	98	65 *Millions of*
Upper	*Lower*	*Middle*	*Upper*	*Lower*	*Upper*	*years ago (mya)*
TRIASSIC		JURASSIC			CRETACEOUS	

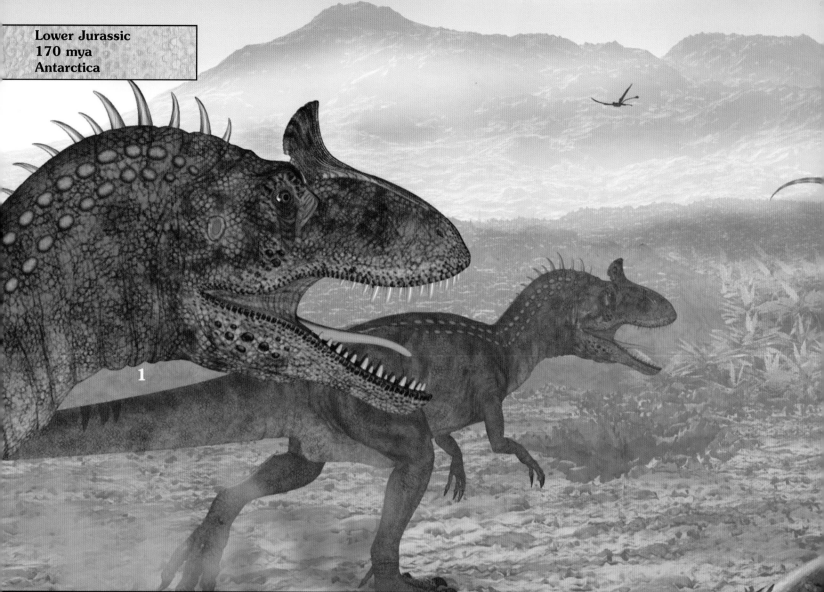

Antarctica

In the temperate Antarctic of the Lower Jurassic, dinosaurs and other animals lived in a climate where temperatures would rarely drop below freezing. *Cryolophosaurus*, a **theropod** dinosaur with an unusual crest, was one of the top **predators**.

Cryolophosaurus was related to *Dilophosaurus* (see pages 20–21). Its strange-looking crest was probably for display. Its mouth was crowded with sharp, serrated teeth, ideal for slicing through flesh. It probably

6

A pair of Cryolophosauruses (1) *launch an attack on a* Glacialisaurus (2). *In the foreground, small* Tritylodons (3) *scamper over an old fallen tree trunk. Above, small pterosaurs (4) take to the sky.*

hunted *Glacialisaurus*, a **sauropodomorph** dinosaur that grew up to 25 feet (7.6 m) long. These long-necked plant eaters would have been easy prey to a fully grown *Cryolophosaurus*. Small mammal-like reptiles called *Tritylodons* were present at the same time. These animals ate plants, burrowing underground for roots. Above them flew pterosaurs.

Cryolophosaurus grew up to 26 feet (8 m) long and weighed around 2,000 pounds (908 kg).

7

European Riverbank

Sarcosaurus was one of the Lower Jurassic's predators living in what is today Europe. Although small for a **carnivore**, it was probably a ferocious hunter. Only part of its skeleton has been found, so scientists are unsure to which group of theropods it belonged.

Armored plant eaters such as *Scelidosaurus* shared the habitat with *Sarcosaurus*. These early **ankylosaurids** had thick skin with rows of bone-like protrusions called scutes or osteoderms sticking out of their

On the bank of a river, a small herd of Scelidosauruses (1) *move down to drink from the river. Watching from high above on the opposite bank are a pair of* Sarcosauruses (2). *They have disturbed a flock of* Dimorphodons (3) *who are feeding on insects.*

backs, necks, and tails. They walked on four legs and ate the softer parts of plants such as the leaves and fruits. Flying above them were *Dimorphodons.* These pterosaurs had a wingspan of 4.6 feet (1.40 m) and a long tail with a small vane. Their large heads had jaws with large, fang-like teeth that projected forward. These were ideal for catching insects and lizards.

Sarcosaurus grew up to 11 feet (3.4 m) long and weighed around 500 pounds (227 kg).

1

Hunting Dragons

Lophostropheus was an early theropod living in what is now Europe about 200–196 million years ago. It was a medium-sized carnivore preying on small plant-eating dinosaurs like *Pantydraco*.

Pantydraco, meaning "**Pant-y-ffynnon** dragon," was a 6-foot (1.8 m) long **omnivore** that lived in the woodlands of what is now western Europe. It ate mainly plants but would have eaten small lizards and insects when it got the chance. It could run on two legs to escape

10

A pair of Lophostropheus (1) *carnivores have found a group of* Pantydracos (2) *feeding on the thick vegetation growing on the edge of a cliff. Above them,* Campylognathoides (3) *glide on an updraft of air.*

hunters such as *Lophostropheus*. In the air above and in the woodlands flew various pterosaurs. Living at the same time as *Dorygnathus* (see pages 12–13) were *Campylognathoides*. They had a wingspan of 5 feet (1.5 m), and their teeth show that they were adapted to eating small lizards and insects.

Lophostropheus was about 20 feet (6.1 m) long and weighed around 500 pounds (227 kg).

1

Pterosaur Colony

It is possible that some pterosaurs had similar lifestyles to today's seabirds. They may have lived in colonies on the steep sides of cliffs. **Fossils** of both *Dorygnathus* and *Parapsicephalus* have been found far out at sea, suggesting their search for food took them many miles.

Dorygnathus had an elongated skull with long jaws that were crowded with 44 needle-sharp teeth. The front teeth were long and pointed forward, which made a perfect gripping device for catching and holding

On the cliffs of an island in what is today part of Europe, two types of pterosaurs Dorygnathus (1) and Parapsicephalus (2) compete with each other for fish in the Tethys Sea. Moving in on their feeding grounds are a pair of Attenborosauruses (3).

on to slippery fish. It may have caught its meal by gliding above the water and plucking out small fish that swam close to the surface. *Parapsicephalus* was a long-tailed pterosaur with smaller teeth than *Dorygnathus*. It would have competed for fish with its close relative. Feeding in the same area were long-necked plesiosaurs such as *Attenborosaurus*.

Both *Dorygnathus* and *Parapsicephalus* were similar in size, each with a wingspan of 3.3 feet (1 m).

13

1

Long-Neck Monsters

The seas of the Lower Jurassic recovered from the mass extinction event at the end of the Triassic period. Large marine reptiles began to flourish, feeding on the large variety of sea life that included fish, sea turtles, **belemnites**, and **ammonites**.

Some of these reptiles had long necks and flippers. They were members of the **sauropterygians**, meaning "lizard flippers." The plesiosaurs were the only member of this group that survived the

A Plesiosaurus (1) *chases after a school of sharks in the part of the Tethys Sea that is now Europe. In the distance, a* **pliosaur** *called* Macroplata (2) *follows a school of fish. Between them swims a larger pliosaur,* Rhomaleosaurus (3).

extinction event. Alongside them swam a new group that looked similar called the pliosaurs. *Plesiosaurus* used its sharp teeth like a fish trap. It swam using its flippers. Its neck could have been used as a rudder during a chase. Pliosaurs like *Rhomaleosaurus* and *Macroplata* fed on ichthyosaurs (see pages 16–17), ammonites, and other plesiosaurs. *Macroplata* had powerful front flippers, which meant it could swim very fast.

Plesiosaurus grew up to 16 feet (4.9 m) long and weighed about 1,000 pounds (454 kg).

15

4

5

3

Ocean Hunters

Like the plesiosaurs, the ichthyosaurs survived the end-Triassic extinction event. These speedy marine reptiles were similar to dolphins today. They had dorsal fins and fish-like tails to propel them through the water. Like dolphins, they had to come to the surface to breathe.

It has been estimated that ichthyosaurs could swim at speeds up to 25 mph (40 km/h). Some ichthyosaurs, like *Temnodontosaurus*, appear to have been deep divers, like some modern whales. Scientists think

Along a coral reef, three Stenopterygiuses (1) *chase after fish. A* Kayentachelys (2) *swims for its life. A pair of* Ichthyosauruses (3) *hunt down sharks while a giant relative,* Temnodontosaurus (4), *eats a shark. Pterosaurs (5) snatch fish from above.*

that ichthyosaurs, such as *Ichthyosaurus*, were warm blooded, similar to mammals. Unlike dinosaurs, ichthyosaurs gave birth to live young. Typical ichthyosaurs had very large eyes, protected within a bony ring, suggesting that they may have hunted at night. Ichthyosaurs ranged widely in size. The 40-foot (12 m) *Temnodontosaurus* had the largest eyes of any known vertebrate, at 8 inches (20 cm) in diameter.

Stenopterygius grew up to 13 feet (4 m) long and weighed around 1 ton (907 kg).

1

3

Water Lands

Anchisaurus was one of the first dinosaurs to be discovered in North America. It was probably a plant eater, although scientists think it may also have eaten meat. It was a member of the sauropodomorphs and had many characteristics of a **prosauropod**.

Although it was not itself a prosauropod, *Anchisaurus* was mostly typical of this group. Its teeth were shaped like spoons to rip leaves from branches. It would have spent most of its time on four legs but

18

On the banks of a river, a group of Anchisauruses (1) *feed on the lush plants. A pair turn to face the the threat of a* Protosuchus (2) *emerging from the undergrowth. In the foreground, a* Dinnebitodon (3) *keeps a wary eye out for predators.*

could have reared up on its hind legs to reach higher plants. *Anchisaurus* swallowed gastroliths (gizzard stones) to help break down the food in its stomach. Predators such as *Protosuchus* may have preyed on *Anchisaurus*. This **crocodylomorph** had a double row of bony plates along its back. It was a fast runner and a good swimmer. It may also have preyed on *Dinnebitodon*, which was a small, plant-eating **cynodont**.

Anchisaurus was about 6.6 feet (2 m) long and would have weighed around 60 pounds (27 kg).

The Wet Season

Dilophosaurus, meaning "two-crested lizard," was probably the largest predator of its environment. The teeth of *Dilophosaurus* are long, but the front part of its upper jaw had a gap in it. **Paleontologists** suggest that its jaws may have been too weak to kill large prey. Instead, it may have killed its prey with its claws.

Typical prey for *Dilophosaurus* would have been plant-eating dinosaurs such as *Seitaad*. Fossils of this prosauropod were found in

20

Rain falls on a tropical beach that is now North America. A pair of Dilophosauruses (1) *chase after different prey.* Rhamphinions (2) *take to the air, while two* Seitaads (3) *run for their lives. A small* Scutellosaurus (4) *goes unnoticed behind a fallen tree.*

what appeared to be a collapsed sand dune. Other plant eaters such as *Scutellosaurus* were probably at risk too, although this little dinosaur had armored spikes and studs down its back and tail. Its back legs were longer than its front legs, but scientists think it walked on all fours. However, it may have run on its back legs to escape predators.

Dilophosaurus was about 20 feet (6 m) long and weighed around 1,000 pounds (454 kg).

21

African Desert

In the hot, **arid** conditions of what is today South Africa lived a small plant-eating dinosaur called *Lesothosaurus*. It had long legs, small arms, and a slender tail, suggesting that it was a fast runner.

It had a short, pointed nose, and the lower jaw ended in a beak. Its teeth were sharp and pointed like arrowheads, which would have been ideal for chewing tough plant matter. Living at the same time was a much larger plant eater. The creature was more than 26 feet (8 m)

In the hot interior of Gondwana, a family of Lesothosauruses (1) *make their way to shaded feeding grounds. Two* Aardonyx (2) *walk along the edge of the desert as they pass a* Vulcanodon (3).

long and weighed over half a ton (454 kg). Its name was *Aardonyx.* Most of the time, *Aardonyx* walked upright, but the shape of its front leg bones shows that they were able to take weight, suggesting that sometimes it would drop to all fours. One of the earliest **sauropods**, *Vulcanodon* weighed up to 4 tons (3.6 metric tons). This giant also fed on plants.

Lesothosaurus was 3.3 feet (1 m) long and weighed 8 pounds (3.6 kg).

Southern Forest

The hot interior part of Gondwana, which is now
Africa, had a landscape of deserts and conifer forests.
Living here was a strange-looking dinosaur called
Massospondylus. It was probably a plant eater, and it
walked on two legs, although it would rest on all fours.

Massospondylus possessed a slender body and long neck. Its arms
were shorter than its legs, and it had a large thumb spike that
scientists think it used for feeding and in self-defense. Living alongside

24

A group of Massospondyluses (1) *feed in the shade of a conifer forest in what is today Africa. The peace is shattered by several* Heterodontosauruses (2) *fleeing along a shallow riverbed from a hungry* Syntarsus, *now called* Megapnosaurus (3).

Massospondylus was the small, carnivorous *Megapnosaurus*. This 10-foot (3 m) long predator ran on two legs and hunted smaller dinosaurs such as *Heterodontosaurus*. These were small, fleet-footed **ornithischian** dinosaurs that reached a maximum size of about 3.3 feet (1 m) in length. They were plant eaters with small, tusk-like teeth that stuck out the sides of their mouths.

Massospondylus was around 16 feet (5 m) long and weighed 300 pounds (136 kg).

25

Indian Rockfall

Fossils of one of the earliest sauropod dinosaurs were found in India. Its name was *Barapasaurus,* and the fossils show that even the early sauropods were giants. This plant eater used its long neck to feed on the branches of the tallest trees.

These giants probably lived in herds and, once fully grown, had no fear of predators, as no carnivores of the time were big enough to threaten them. Another early sauropod of the period was *Kotasaurus.*

A Barapasaurus (1) *becomes the victim of a rock fall on the steep slopes of a hill overlooking the coast of what is today India. A Kotasaurus (2) has climbed onto a large rock to avoid the danger. A Dandakosaurus (3) will feed on the carcass later.*

At 30 feet (9 m) long, it was not as large as *Barapasaurus* but probably had a similar lifestyle. These sauropods lived alongside prosauropods such as *Lamplughsaura*. Carnivores such as *Dandakosaurus* reached a length of 10 feet (3 m) and preyed on the smaller prosauropods. However, they might have supplemented their diet on the **carcasses** of sauropods that had died from accidents.

Barapasaurus was about 59 feet (18 m) long and weighed around 53 tons (48 metric tons).

Dinosaurs in China

In the Northern Hemisphere, in what is called Eurasia, dinosaurs roamed amongst the forests and deserts. Here we find the ever-present prosauropods similar to those in the Southern Hemisphere. Fossil finds of several *Yunnanosauruses* in China show that these dinosaurs lived in herds.

Yunnanosaurus had more than sixty spoon-shaped teeth in its jaws, which were self-sharpening as they rubbed against each other when it ate.

28

A small herd of Yunnanosauruses (1) *run for their lives from a* Dilophosaurus (2) *at the edge of a desert in what is now part of China. In the foreground, a small* Bienosaurus (3) *looks up from feeding on a cycad.*

Fossil remains of a *Dilophosaurus* (see pages 20–21) have also been found with those of *Yunnanosaurus,* suggesting that they were preyed upon by this carnivorous theropod. Other dinosaurs roaming the landscape were the very similar prosauropod *Lufengosaurus* and the armored *Bienosaurus.* This small plant eater had boney scutes protuding from its body, neck, and tail that gave it protection from hungry predators.

Yunnanosaurus grew up to 23 feet (7 m) long and weighed around 1 ton (907 kg).

Animal Listing

Other dinosaurs and animals that appear in the scenes.

Aardonyx
(pp. 22–23)
Prosauropod
dinosaur
20 feet (6 m) long
Africa

Attenborosaurus
(pp. 12–13)
Plesiosaur
16 feet (5 m) long
Europe

Bienosaurus
(pp. 28–29)
Ankylosaurid
3.3 feet (1 m) long
Asia

Campylognathoides
(pp. 10–11)
Pterosaur
5-foot (1.5 m)
wingspan
Europe

Dandakosaurus
(pp. 26–27)
Prosauropod
dinosaur
10 feet (3 m) long
India

Dimorphodon
(pp. 8–9)
Pterosaur
4.6-foot (1.4 m)
wingspan
Europe

Dinnebitodon
(pp. 18–19)
Cynodont
6 inches (15 cm)
long
North America

Glacialisaurus
(pp. 6–7)
Sauropodomorph
dinosaur
25 feet (7.6 m) long
Antarctica

Heterodontosaurus
(pp. 24–25)
Ornithischian
dinosaur
3.3 feet (1 m) long
Africa

Ichthyosaurus
(pp. 16–17)
Ichthyosaur
6.5 feet (2 m) long
Europe

Kayentachelys
(pp. 16–17)
Turtle
2 feet (0.6 m) long
North America

Kotasaurus
(pp. 26–27)
Sauropod
30 feet (9 m) long
India

Macroplata
(pp. 14–15)
Pliosaur
15 feet (4.6 m) long
Europe

Megapnosaurus
(pp. 24–25)
Theropod dinosaur
10 feet (3 m) long
Africa

Pantydraco
(pp. 10–11)
Sauropodomorph
dinosaur
6 feet (1.8 m) long
Europe

Protosuchus
(pp. 18–19)
Crocodylomorph
3.3 feet (1 m) long
North America

Rhamphinion
(pp. 20–21)
Pterosaur
4.9-foot (1.5 m)
wingspan
North America

Rhomaleosaurus
(pp. 14–15)
Pliosaur
23 feet (7 m) long
Europe

Scelidosaurus
(pp. 8–9)
Armored dinosaur
13 feet (4 m) long
Europe, North
America

Scutellosaurus
(pp. 20–21)
Armored dinosaur
3.9 feet (1.2 m) long
North America

Seitaad
(pp. 20–21)
Prosauropod
dinosaur
15 feet (4.6 m) long
North America

Temnodontosaurus
(pp. 16–17)
Ichthyosaur
40 feet (12 m) long
Europe

Tritylodon
(pp. 6–7)
Tritylodont
1 foot (0.3 m) long
Africa, Antarctica

Vulcanodon
(pp. 22–23)
Sauropod dinosaur
20 feet (6 m) long
Africa

Glossary

ammonite An extinct marine animal with a shell that looks similar to today's nautilus.

ankylosaurid A member of the *Ankylosaurus* family of armored, plant-eating dinosaurs.

arid Very dry, with little or no water.

belemnites Squid-like sea creatures.

carcasses The bodies of dead animals.

carnivores Meat-eating animals.

crocodylomorph A group of animals that include crocodilians and their extinct relatives.

cycad A kind of palm.

cynodonts A group of therapsids with mammal-like features that laid eggs.

fossils The remains of living things that have turned to rock.

ginkgo An unusual nonflowering plant that is regarded as a living fossil that first appeared in the Lower Jurassic.

ichthyosaur A sea reptile that resembled fish and dolphins.

mass extinction event A large-scale disappearance of species of animals and plants in a relatively short period of time.

monkey puzzle tree An evergreen tree growing to 130 feet (40 m) tall with tough, scale-like, triangular leaves.

omnivore An animal that eats both plants and animals.

ornithischian Bird-hipped dinosaur.

paleontologist A scientist who studies the forms of life that existed in earlier geologic periods by looking at fossils.

Pant-y-ffynnon A village in South Wales, United Kingdom.

plesiosaur Marine reptiles with long necks and flippers.

pliosaur Marine reptiles related to the true plesiosaurs.

predator An animal that hunts and kills other animals for food.

prosauropod A member of a group of long-necked, herbivorous dinosaurs that eventually dropped down on all fours and became sauropods.

pterosaur A flying reptile.

sauropod A member of a group of large plant-eating dinosaurs that had very long necks.

sauropodomorph A member of the group of long-necked dinosaurs that includes prosauropods and sauropods.

sauropterygian A member of the group of aquatic reptiles that includes plesiosaurs.

temperate Region where seasonal changes are not extreme.

theropod A member of a two-legged dinosaur family that included most of the giant carnivorous dinosaurs.

Index